Thus Spoke Moti

Copyright © 2019 by J.A. Patrina.

All rights reserved. No part of this book may be reproduced in any form or by any electronic or mechanical means, including information storage and retrieval systems, without permission in writing from the publisher, except by reviewers, who may quote brief passages in a review.

This publication contains the opinions and ideas of its author. It is intended to provide helpful and informative material on the subjects addressed in the publication. The authors and publisher specifically disclaim all responsibility for any liability, loss, or risk, personal or otherwise, which is incurred as a consequence, directly or indirectly, of the use and application of any of the contents of this book.

ISBN: 978-1-7330672-0-1   [Paperback Edition]

Printed and bound in The United States of America.

Published by LittleHouse Enterprises Inc.

Introduction

For some time, I have been researching ancient texts trying to envision what really happened in the early days of mankind. As most of the source material comes out of a religious corner – e.g. The Bible - I trained myself to ignore the divinity overtones and to just extrapolate the historical content of whatever I read.

In 2016, I decided to begin work on a book titled: *Subjugated*, which includes the saga of Joshua's conquest of the promised land. As I had never been to Israel, I felt now the moment to go, prior to putting time into such an endeavor.

This booklet, *Notes from Israel*, is a travelogue, the reconnaissance trip taking place the last week of December, 2016. It is written for anyone who wants the low down on the region's dimensions: geography, ancient and modern history, racial makeup, religious practices, the myths, legends and any evidence one can encounter only by being there.

Luckily I picked the right guide.

Enjoy this eye opener.

J.A. Patrina
January 5, 2017

Moti

Guess which one is Moti.

What a break getting "professor" Moti as our guide for four days in Israel. With my wife and two daughters planted in the back seat and me up front, we crisscross Israel, on-and-off road, in his Land Rover, with Moti doing most of the talking.

Everything gets covered, the history of mankind plus Moti's whole life. A year younger than me, Moti's story mirrors many baby-boomer Jews: parents surviving World War II and flocking to Israel, their children – e.g. Moti - going to war multiple times to preserve their new promised land.

A retired officer, Moti's Sinai dessert tank crew had 21 kills against Egypt during the 1973 Yom Kipper War. Since military retirement 25 years ago, Moti throws himself into touring, basking with joy in presenting Israel's every nook and cranny, especially to people like us coming from the motherland, America.

Moti: *Israel is the 51st state.*

Moti knows almost as much about America as I do, implying that it's about time I visit the only American outpost further from the heartland than Hawaii.

Moti: *Obama doesn't hate Israel; he just hates Netanyahu because Netanyahu is not socialist.*

Note: In 2016, Obama signed off on a 20 billion, five-year commitment to finance Israel's military, though Obama had just infused both Democrat Party operatives and cash into Israel's leftist party to stop Netanyahu's re-election. I wonder who really hacked the U.S. Democrat Party's emails.

Slowly I piece together the avalanche of information Moti throws at me. He can tell I'm a sponge for history, and he strategizes the four days we have to cover 6,000 years of people killing each other. To start, one must know who these people were and are.

Jews

Let's begin with the Jews, of which there are at least seven types:

1. Regular Patriotic Israelis like Moti, mainly living in Tel Aviv and on the coast, who, though patriotic, are not hot heads about their disdain for Muslim Arabs; they simply can't stand them. The lack of Muslim productivity, the filth and brutishness of these people drive the Israelis' nuts.

Moti: *Don't refer to that garbage you see there (down a Muslim street) as garbage. That, offends them. Call it flowers. And: If you see trees, that's Jewish land, no trees, Arab land. They don't plant things; they don't do anything! In Gaza unemployment is at 90% and they don't teach their children anything but hate, so how can they ever work? Instead, we build the walls and they dig tunnels.*

2. Extremist Settlers, the one's that set-up "in your face" barbed-wired, fenced-in "settlements" right inside Arab-dominated West Bank territory.

Moti: *For years, Rome left the Jews alone under Herod until the Zealots went too far, and then everyone died. These settlers are our Zealots; they put us all in danger. They're so extreme that they would shoot Israelis soldiers if the government tried to shut down their settlement.*

3. Kibbutz Members, the original founders of the 1948 era socialist farming cooperatives where shoulder-to-shoulder, everyone shared in the prosperity of their Kibbutz.

Moti: *These people do not work. They are so rich that they hire others to do everything. They got the land for free sixty years ago and now it's worth a fortune.*

4. Ethiopian Jews, refugees from Africa.

Moti: *Any Jew anywhere is welcome to live here; It's their birth right. Until they got here the Ethiopian refuges did not live in houses. Now we give them housing.*

5. Rich American Jews, who are always visiting Israel.

Moti: *They all have money, and without it Israel would die.*

6. Orthodox Jews, who believe the words of the Torah were dictated by God to Moses. 'Orthodox' Judaism does not tolerate varieties of Judaism. Rules are rules.

Moti: *These people are basically ok.*

7. Hasidic Jews, a subset of Orthodoxy, parasites, the worst, everyone hates them, living in Jerusalem near the Wailing Wall, their spot.

Moti: *The men do not work, period. They spend all day studying the Torah (first five books of the bible), making their slave wives do everything. They all have seven children while living off of everyone else in Israel.*

When I ask how the Hasidic get away with this Moti explains:

Moti: *First, they believe they stand closer to God than all other people on earth; everyone else is a sinner, deserving nothing. Second, tell me, what percent of America votes? Maybe half? Well the Hasidics are just 10%, but they all vote 101%, giving them 20% of the Knesset (Israel's parliament). Even dead Hasidics vote! There, see that poster. That's their Rabbi; he calls the shots and the whole bunch vote like robots.*

I cut in still wondering how Hasidics feed themselves.

Moti: *Why does America have just two political parties; I never understood it! In Israel we have ten parties and to form a government the party with the most votes always has to come to the Hasidics to form a majority. And the Hasidics hate them all but will join anyone as long as welfare monies are guaranteed. It's blackmail.*

I got it, but he continues.

Moti: *And they have all of these children. Soon they will be 20%, getting them 40% of the Knesset, bleeding Israel dry.*

Note 1: In 2010 a report released by the Israel Central Bureau of Statistics showed that **8%** of Israel's Jewish population defines itself as ultra-Orthodox, **12%** as Orthodox, **13%** as traditional-religious, **25%** as traditional, and **42%** as secular, on a descending scale of religiosity.

Note 2: My own experience with 7 Hasidic Jews in America – the Brooklyn NY Hasidics - has been with men who have real businesses.

Arabs

Understanding the Arabs comes next, four basic types:

1. Muslim Arabs (Palistinians) - 5.6 million of them – mainly living in the "West Bank" and Gaza Strip areas. These are the areas taken by Israel in 1967 during the Six-day War. One day, five Arab countries of 30 million people attacked Israel's 600,000 people, and Israel crushed the various Arab armies in six days, go figure.

In victory Israel grabbed a bit more land to provide a more reasonable geographic buffer between themselves and the aggressors. Today, Tel Aviv is 40 miles from Jordan and not 20 miles as it once stood.

Moti: *Do not call them Palestinians, they are not from what you think of as Palestine. They are Arabs who recently moved into "Palestine" to live off the growing economy of Israel. I am a Jew living in Palestine. I am a Palestinian.*

Moti: *In 1948 there were 150,000 Arabs in "Palestine", now there are millions, with more coming in daily. Why not, they get free medical. Yasser Arafat was not "Palestinian"; he was a terrorist from Egypt making himself king of the "Palestinians", a refuge people deserted by other Arabs in Egypt and Jordan with no place to go.*

2. Christian Arabs – Maybe 20,000, mostly living in Bethlehem and leaving Israel in droves.

Moti: *Christian Arabs are moral people, with values and manners, but they are overwhelmed by the Muslims surrounding them which is why they are leaving. They should have joined Israel after 1967 before the Muslims moved into Bethlehem, but they didn't, and now they see what you get living with Muslims for almost fifty years.*

3. Bedouin Arabs – Maybe 200,000 – living in the desert regions of Israel with their Sheiks, camels, goats, donkeys, sheep and head gear.

Moti: *These Arabs no longer wander, living in tents; they have fixed territories now and live in shacks with garbage all around them.*

If you touch a Bedouin girl, she is killed. To marry a Bedouin, you must give the father 10,000, and he gives a percentage to his Sheik. If you are a Sheik you can exchange one of your young daughters for the young daughter of another Sheik, and no money changes hands. They have a whole system.

> *When I was divorced I met a beautiful Bedouin girl. She would tell me things she wanted and I would buy them for her. I considered marrying her, but realized I would be married to her tribe.*

4. Chechens – 40,000 - Actually Muslim, but loyal to Israel.

Moti: *These people are from central Asia, central Asians living in Palestine. So that makes them "Palestinians" like all the rest of us. See that shiny Mosque on the hill, it's only two years old. A billionaire from Chechenia paid for it.*

Note: *In Israel, though everyone is a "Palestinian", "Palestinian" Arabs cannot vote, nor can they join the military. So there are two classes of Israelis in "Palestine". That's the rub.*

And so, as we travel through the country attempting to dig into historical subjects, these Jewish/Arab constituents always come up… and how could they not. The highways are walled whenever passing an Arab town, some of the walls extremely high.

Moti: *Those extensions to the wall… they shield cars from Arab snipers living up in the high rises.*

Moti: *See that salt factory on the shoreline (*of the dead sea*), the Kibbutz owns it and brings in 200 million a year with only 50 members.*

Next up: Masada (above), King Herod's desert fortress.

Masada

Masada sits overlooking the dead sea. 2,000 years ago it was the last stand of the mentioned Zealots who had egged the Romans on starting in 66 AD. This uprising led to the end of Israel for the next two millenniums, hence Moti's distrust of today's edgy West Bank Settlers.

After the Zealot-led riots in Jerusalem, Rome slaughtered everyone, the guilty and the innocent, leveling Jerusalem and its gigantic temple. A point was being made. Some of the Zealots fled to the Masada desert fortress built 50-years prior by King Herod (the one that did Jesus in).

Masada is a rock formation 1,300 feet high, with a plateau on top and sheer cliff walls all around. Herod built it as a self-contained refuge, boasting warehouses to hold multiple years of food and a self-filling cistern system for collecting water.

In 70 AD, when the Zealots went to Masada, a Roman garrison occupied it. No one knows how the Zealots got in, but they took the complex.

A second Roman unit sent to drive the Zealots from Masada are somehow destroyed as well. A humiliated Roman Emperor orders a full legion in, and that does the trick. The plateau is surrounded so that Zealots cannot slip out, and the Roman general orders a dirt ramp built of Herculean proportions, a road to the top.

A few months later all is ready and the Romans knock down a section of the upper defense wall with a siege fortress pushed to the top. Upon entry the Zealots are found dead except for one woman who serves as witness:

> *Each zealot first kills his own family, then ten zealots selected by lottery kill the men, and one zealot, again by lottery, kills the nine and falls on his sword to finish it off.*

As we say in America "Live free or die".

Moti: *When I entered the army at 19, we climbed the snake* (Masada's foot path) *in the heat, some of the boys collapsing along the way. We were sworn in to defend Israel with our lives right here where the wall was breached.*

BTW, my wife and daughters climbed Masada while Moti and I had Cappuccinos, taking the tram up.

Coming back from Masada we see 50 or more camels moving about in a rare area of vegetation sitting between the road and the Dead Sea. Moti explains the presence of trees and bushes saying that water from distant mountains leaches through the sandstone range, finding its way out here, hence the growth. We are thrilled to see the animals.

Moti: *Those camels belong to the Sheik. They are down here grazing for the winter. A Sheik's reputation grows based on how may camels he has.*

Moti: *Camels are smart. When I was an officer in the Sinai, beside tanks, we had 30 camels assigned to us. One day I am told a camel is stuck in a kind of quick sand. We bring a rope and a truck and the truck gets stuck. We extract the truck with one of our tanks. Finally, a Bedouin comes up laughing at us saying he can get the camel out. How I ask. You will see, no more questions. The Bedouin grabs a three-foot stick and moves towards the camel while making a sound like an animal. As he nears the quick sand the camel gets up and pushes himself out to avoid the stick. You see, camels are smart, he sat in the sand to stay cool, and knew when to get out.*

Moti, also while driving along the Dead Sea: *Here is where the Ibex deer live. By now (twilight) they are up hiding from the leopard, but the last leopard around here died a few months ago, hit by a bus. Now it's just jackals.*

The Dead Sea

The Dead Sea is dying; I think?

It looks half empty, the water's edge far away, circled by empty stretches of barren land where water recently stood.

Moti: *When I was a boy, my father brought me to Masada for my Bar Mitzvah and all of this was water. It's the fault of the salt factories. They pump water out, let it evaporate in pools and then harvest the dried salts and minerals. The level goes down each year.*

This upsets me and I say so.

Moti: *There is a plan to run sea water a 150 kilometers from the Red Sea to here.*

I wonder how much gravity is envisioned.

Moti: *We are 400 meters below sea level. That's plenty to get the water here and plenty to make electricity.*

I envision an endless string of turban generators generating power all the way down the line.

Moti: *Problem is, half the Dead Sea is in Jordan, so we will need to partner with them.*

I get excited at the prospects for such a project: save the Dead Sea, make pollution-free electricity forever, and bring these two close friends – Israel and Jordan – even closer together.

Moti: *So far no one has agreed to build it for free, the way oil companies build pipelines for free to get the oil out. But we'll see.*

I suggest Jordan and Israel each float five billion in 100-year revenue bonds at 6%, with a 1% principle pay down annually. The annual principle plus interest to be offset by electricity revenues. Moti likes it.

Moti: *Of course it could rain. In Roman times the water level is where it is now, but it came up by the time I was a boy, so it can come up again.*

Next up Joshua conquers Jericho.

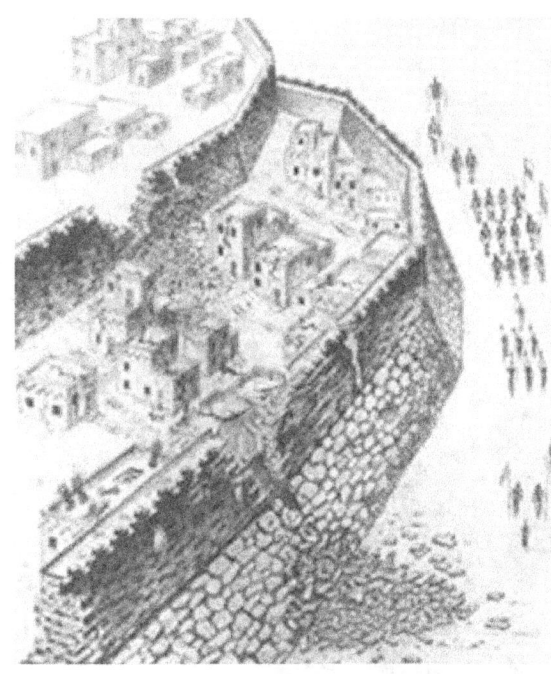

Hebrews circling Jericho with the Ark

Jericho

Joshua at the head of forty thousand Hebrews, in 120-degree heat.

My main purpose for the trip centered around research for the book I am writing about the conquest of the promised land by the Israelites. Back in the day, after Moses handed the reins over to Joshua, the bible cites Joshua defeating

32 Canaanite kingdoms in seven years, the most famous victory coming at Jericho.

Some declare Jericho the oldest city in the world (though probably not true).

Monastery built into the mountain

Jericho offered three advantages to the ancients: first, *Elisha's Spring* comes out of the mountains - like the one Moti already described when we spied the camel herd – and second, the *Jordan River* flows past it emptying into the Dead Sea. But third, *Temptation Mountain* sits due west behind the city. In the late afternoon the mountain shades the area hours before sunset providing early relief to the city.

This is the mountain where, supposedly, the devil tempted Jesus before Jesus was baptized in the near-by Jordan River.

Before Jericho's destruction, the stretch of land between the city and the river was fully cultivated, a vast green oasis amongst the brown desert landscape.

But to win the promised land - wanting to crush dozens more kingdoms after dispatching Jericho - Joshua needed to stay on a tight schedule. Long sieges were out, and this is where the Arc of the Covenant comes in. The Arc, besides holding the ten commandments, held something more, probably an anti-gravity mechanism.

When activated, the anti-gravity energy destabilized the local gravity waves emanating from the earth. The Red Sea would part. Locust would swarm, hornets could be herded into the faces of one's enemies, etc....

At Jericho, the Arc did two things: first, it arrested the water coming down the Jordan River so that the Israelis hoard, forty thousand strong, could cross and make camp inside the Oasis on the Jericho side, and second (mainly), to either destabilize the walls and buildings of the city in order to collapse them, or cause a localized earth quake.

They achieved a collapse by marching the Arc around the city for seven days building an anti-gravity field that either a) soon compromised the molecular cohesion of the bricks or b) weakened the earth's foundation crust via quake. When it all went down the Israelis soldiers picked through the rubble to finish off any Canaanite not already crushed.

After Jericho, Joshua and the boys took 32 other Canaanite principalities inside the "promised land", wiping out 99% of the population, afterwards dividing the land by lot, between the twelve tribes of Israel.

Few people realize that some of those killed were giants anywhere from eight to twelve feet in stature, like King Og, whose bed was 15 feet long.

(Sumerian Carving)

According to the bible, these were a leftover cross-breed of humans that towered over normal humans. Most of the Canaanite Kings, the giants, went down for the count as well, though some survived. David killed Goliath – 9 ½ feet – 400 years later.

Skeleton discovered in Hungary. Hmm…

Note: *The above sections are a peak into "Subjugated", the mentioned book I am writing.*

Moti: *Ok say goodbye to Jericho, let's go to the river where John baptized Jesus.*

The Jordan River

We find the baptismal site down the road a bit, the Jordan River now but a stream. I wonder why the Arc was needed to cross it. Below, the Jordan empties into the Dead sea.

Moti: *Further north is the Sea of Galilee, which, like the Dead Sea, is half empty for the same reasons: not as much rain now as in the "milk and honey" days, plus today river water is diverted for irrigation. So this is what you get.*

Pointing east to a mountain on the Jordanian side of the Dead Sea, Moti adds: *Herod, our great builder, had another palace fortress up on that mountain. This is where they cut the head off* (of John the Baptist).

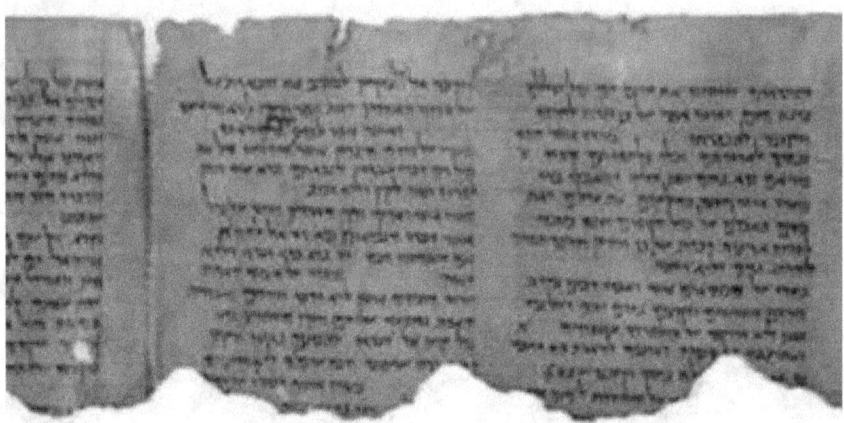

That about covered the Jordan River and John the Baptist so we moved on, headed to a local Kibbutz for lunch. On the way Moti points to some caves up on a cliff:

Moti: *That's where the Dead Sea scrolls were found by some Bedouins. The theory is that in 70 AD, when Rome came in to destroy Jerusalem, the Rabbis' took the temple scrolls hid them here.*

The Kibbutz

When Moti retired from the army he lived on a Kibbutz overlooking the Dead Sea. This is when he met the Bedouin girl he didn't marry.

A few years later he met an Israelis girl, married her, and it didn't take long for the new wife to put her foot down about living in a Kibbutz, so they moved to Jerusalem and set up house. Moti talked about his wife often, so the move worked out.

But once a desert boy always a desert boy, and Moti still dreams of desert life on the Kibbutz. No wonder he looks forward to bring visitors out here each day.

Moti: *See all of these palm and date groves, they belong to the Kibbutz. The disadvantage of the desert becomes an advantage if you have access to water. The soil around here is phenomenal, filled with minerals that enrich the fruit. This is why Dead Sea melons and tomatoes are sold all year long around the world.*

Apparently one can go to the Kibbutz and have some sort of lunch. We pull off the road into what looks like a country club with mowed lawns in the desert.

Above, a kibbutz today

Moti: *The people you will see here are not members of the Kibbutz. Kibbutz members do not work. The workers can be Jews or Arab; the Kibbutz does not care as either way, members do not work.*

We pay and get a cafeteria meal, which I devour, and Moti explains further:

Moti: *In the 1950's the new State of Israel gave land away if you wanted to start a Kibbutz. This way the stream of Jews emigrating from everywhere would move out of Tel Aviv and Jerusalem and colonize the land.*

Each family had a share in what their Kibbutz sold from the farm. This was the real socialism; the collective owned the collective's production, not the state, like in Russia. But next, the Kibbutz members had children. What share do they get?

I confess not to know.

Moti: *No one knew, so they had to become capitalists. Member shares became stock shares that could be inherited, gifted or sold. The stockholders got dividends. Today these are businesses; members profit off of the surplus productivity of their workers – just like Marx warned. The socialist Kibbutz does not exist.*

Jerusalem Time Line

Before digging into the old city of Jerusalem, including the Jewish, Christian, Muslim and Armenian quarters, we should spend a page or two reviewing the cities long history.

2,200 BC – or so - Like Jericho, Jerusalem's ancient roots go back a few thousand years BC, also populated by Canaanites, and also housing a few giants.

1,500 BC – or so - Curiously, when Joshua was kicking butt all over the promised land one of the places not taken was Jerusalem: too much resistance from the *Jebuite* people living there and Joshua had to move on. Thirty-two other cities needed to be destroyed and like I said, he didn't do sieges.

In 1,000 BC – or so – *David* kills *Goliath* and becomes the second king of Israel after *King Saul* dies. Before Saul, the twelve tribes operated autonomously on the land allocated to them back in Joshua's day. Once king, David defeats the *Jebuites* still in Jerusalem, he makes Jerusalem his capital.

In 900 BC – or so – *Solomon*, David's son by *Bathsheba*, becomes Israel's third king, and he really gets things going. Enough wealth is created to pay for municipal projects, like the first Temple.

In 600 BC – or so – *King Nebuchadnezzar* of Babylon conquers Jerusalem and burns it to the ground, many Hebrews are taken to Babylon as slaves. Fifty years later the Persian *King Cyrus* conquers Babylon, Jews are allowed to return and Jerusalem is re-built, including the second Temple.

In 325 BC – or so – *Alexander the Great* establishes 200 years of "Hellenization" in the region.

In 125 BC – or so – The Jerusalem region is "left alone" and ruled as the *Hasmonean Kingdom* (whoever they were).

In 50 BC - or so – After being conquered by Rome in 63 BC, *Herod* becomes the "client king of Rome" in Judea. The great builder, besides Masada and like projects, expands the temple and the city, and presides over the crucifixion of *Jesus of Nazareth*.

In 33 AD – Jesus is crucified on Calgary Hill inside Jerusalem.

In 70 AD – Rome destroys the Temple and much of Jerusalem to punish the region for disloyalty and the actions of the Zealots.

In 135 AD – Emperor Hadrian (of Hadrian's wall), orders the construction of what we now call "The Old City", as a pagan city. Jews rebel and Hadrian has hundreds of thousands killed (an amazing number).

In 335 AD – Emperor Constantine converts to Christianity and Jerusalem becomes a Christian center. Jews are banned.

In 638 AD – The Muslim Caliph Umar ibn al-Khattab conquers Jerusalem. The Dome of the Rock is built where Mohammad ascended to Heaven on his white horse.

In 1,099 AD – The Crusaders conquer Jerusalem creating the Kingdom of Jerusalem, and build churches where crucifixion events occurred.

In 1517 AD – The Ottoman Turkish Sultan Suleiman the Magnificent takes over, builds the city walls we see today and permits Jews, Christians and Moslems to worship and dwell in Jerusalem.

In 1917 – Following the defeat of the Ottomans by Great Britain in World War I, British rule begins, called "The British Mandate".

In 1948 – The State of Israel is formed, with David ben Gurion as leader. Israel repels massive Arab armies who attack on the very day independence is declared (a miracle).

In 1956 - Israel, backed by the United Kingdom and France, attacks Egypt over Egypt's nationalization of the Suez Canal.

In 1967 – Five Arab nations swarm and are about to attack Israel. Israel launches preemptive strikes and defeats all comers in what became "the Six Day War".

In 1973 - Arab states again attack Israel on Yom Kippur, with Israel destroying 2,300 Arab tanks in Syria and the Sinai Desert.

Till now – generally – with their armies destroyed, Arab enemies turn to terrorism, via a) declaring Intifadas (holy wars to "shake off" the infidels), and b) by Iran financing both Hezbollah and Hamas on Israel's borders. Many military conflicts ensue, and Israel builds walls in Gaza and in the West Bank to contain Arab agents within their own territories.

Nope, it's never easy!

The Old City

Ok, let's go. Recall that in 1517 AD, the Ottoman Turkish Sultan *Suleiman the Magnificent* built the city walls of Jerusalem. There are various medieval-styled gates in the wall – like the Damascus Gate and the Jaffa Gate - that connect to yesterday's highways.

Shortly we will peek into the four quarters of the old city, but first a word about "true believers" as these types are everywhere once inside the walls.

Abraham Lincoln believed in God, but he did not believe that God interacted with Lincoln other than to create a spirit world that Lincoln was part of – for inspiration and moral direction. Asked about his conception of God, **Lincoln** replied:

> *"The same as my conception of nature.*
> *That it is impossible for either to be personal."*

The opposite is true inside the walls of old Jerusalem. To people in all four quarters, the "God and me" syndrome prevails. Not only can one communicate with God, but through prayer God will alter your destiny on occasion. To learn how to do this, each religion was shown the protocol - by God himself - on how God wants us to interact with him.

Moses defined God's will in the Torah; Jesus defined God's will in the New Testament, and Mohammad defined God's will in the Quran. Yet they have fundamental differences. So either two of the three have it wrong, or possible all three are off base. Of course a theologian could make the sophist argument that God has no rules and all three can be correct.

Whether the people in the old city consider this dilemma I cannot say, but it appears that God's position does not matter, as each believes their "God and me" protocol the divine word, the others infidels. In common, without any evidence whatsoever, all believe God is up there fretting about each and every individual. Millions show up to pursue this personal relationship fantasy. God bless them for trying, and maybe *He* does hear them.

Nevertheless, in the presence of each holy site, one is moved.

Foreground: the Jewish Wailing Wall, Background: The Muslim Dome of the Rock. Snuggle up.

The Christian Quarter

Calgary Hill has had a church complex covering it since the crusades. The spot of the crucifixion is a primitive chapel with many lamps hanging from the ceiling, above a small alter. The devout kiss the alter. Outside the chapel is a stone slab where Jesus laid upon removal from the cross, and the devout kiss this stone. Across from the city, on the opposite hill, the olive grove where Judas betrayed Jesus still grows filled with ancient trees. A church sits on the spot where the betrayal took place. It too has a stone which the devout kiss.

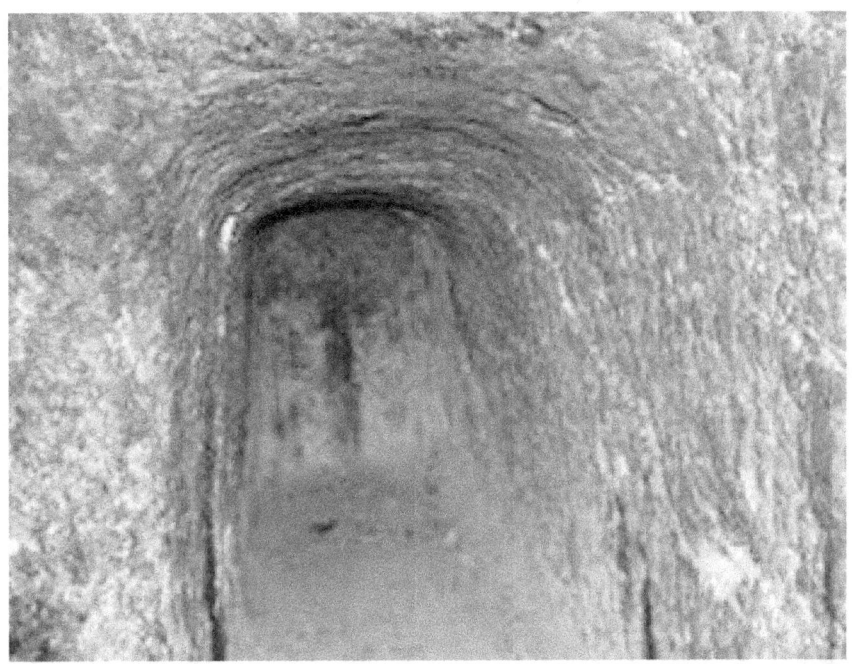

A curious claim, just feet from the crucifixion site, is an overly convenient cave where they say Jesus was buried and the resurrection took place. It is small, and fits one person, so I wonder that no other bodies were already residing there from prior crucifixions.

I surmise the body went elsewhere, but the burial site debate matters not. Resurrection matters.

The Moslem Quarter

Around the corner one finds the Moslem quarter.

After walking down more alleys, there is a side ally - really a tunnel in the buildings - and at the end of the tunnel are steps, maybe seven of them, that lead to an opening. As one nears the steps, through the opening, one sees the gold half circle of the Dome of the Rock, the huge mosque built on the spot where Mohammed ascended to heaven on his white horse. I am told one must be Muslim to go up the stairs and into the mosque area. I ask what would happen if I go up there and am baited "try it and see".

I start up the steps and two older men block the opening and a younger guard comes face to face with me saying "only Muslims."

"Really", I ask feigning disbelief and the guard moves in as close as a boot camp sergeant glaring at me. I pretend not to notice and keep looking at the gold dome. He tries to intensify the stare; I pretend not to notice. Inwardly I speculate that, technically, he has no legal right to stop me, but since this is not my fight I step away. I wonder if this case has come before the Israel supreme court. It probably has.

One thing is for sure, if you want to avoid being nuked, live in the old city. Iran will never target such a consecrated place. Tel Aviv yes, Jerusalem no.

The Jewish Quarter

Next door to the Moslem Quarter one finds the Jewish Quarter just down the alleyway. Instead of Muslim merchants one suddenly finds Jewish merchants selling different kinds of worthless stuff. Wherever you go, the alleys house endless little hole-in-the-wall shops and I wonder how they stay in business, except for the Jewish bakeries which are amazing and filled with customers.

While walking down such an alley, suddenly one falls upon what might be called "wailing wall plaza". It's the size of a couple of football fields, and there it stands, the gigantic *Wailing Wall*, itself a hundred yards wide and 60 feet tall, the surviving western wall of the temple destroyed by Rome in 70 AD – the same temple built in 500 BC by Hebrews returning from Babylon on top of the ruins of Solomon's temple built in 900 BC. I am in awe. Below the men's section.

Once in the wall's presence men and woman must separate, men to the left and woman to the right, the wall itself demarcated by a dividing fence that keep the sexes apart once in its midst.

Entering the receiving plaza one choses a sex-defined ramp leading down to the demarcation area. I chose the male ramp, the girls the female ramp. I said I would meet them back in the general area. Above, the demarcation fence.

At bottom of my ramp, I grab a free yarmulke (skull cap) and place it on my head. A few steps later I am at the wall, together with some Hasidic enthusiasts who bow profusely at the wall, never resting. Tucked within the crevasses of the wall's stone blocs are thousands of paper notes, homages to God by the worshipers. I want to place my message to God but have no paper and have no message.

I watch young men, some from America - bar mitzvah candidates - led by a rabbi and a male entourage of relatives. They carry the Torah around, kept in tabernacles housed to the side of the praying section. I stay for some time watching, feeling I will never be back.

The Armenian Quarter

Don't fret should you not know what or where Armenia is; it's a small country east of Turkey.

Doubting Thomas, the Apostle, brought Christianity there a very long time ago before also traveling to India. Being in the middle of nowhere, Armenian Christianity never got updates from either Rome or Constantinople when important decisions were made. For instance, the Armenians think Christmas on January 25th. What idiots!

So how did they get a quarter of Jerusalem?

Above: Armenian church in Jerusalem

They got there first. Armenia was the first Christian country. They said "yes" ahead of Emperor Constantine of Rome. Armenia promptly sent monks to settle Jerusalem in the early 300's.

The only philosophical difference between Armenian Christians and others stems from the Armenian belief of the "unified" Christ: a blend of divinity and humanity, whereas western Christian doctrine asserts the "duality" of Christ: he separately exists both as a man and as a God – sometimes the man part dominates, like when he turned over the money changer tables in anger. Theology – claiming the attributes of God - is unbelievable!

Anyhow Armenia has their own quarter, and I say: why not?

Bethlehem

Moti next plans Bethlehem, its hill visible from Jerusalem. It is a Muslim-controlled West Bank municipality.

Moti: *I can bring you there, but only Arabs can run the tour. You will need one hundred dollars. I will call and arrange the guide.*

And so we depart for Bethlehem, the road protected from terrorists by walls and cameras.

Moti: *This is your guide Kamil. He will take you in a van to the birth place.*

Kamil, our Palestinian Christian guide in Bethlehem, walks us through the caves where Jesus was born (above).

No one that I know knows that Jesus was born in a cave, a real cave. But now that I have been there I have no doubt that the birth happened in this sunken place. One truly fathoms the dire circumstances from which Christianity blossomed, 2,000 years prior.

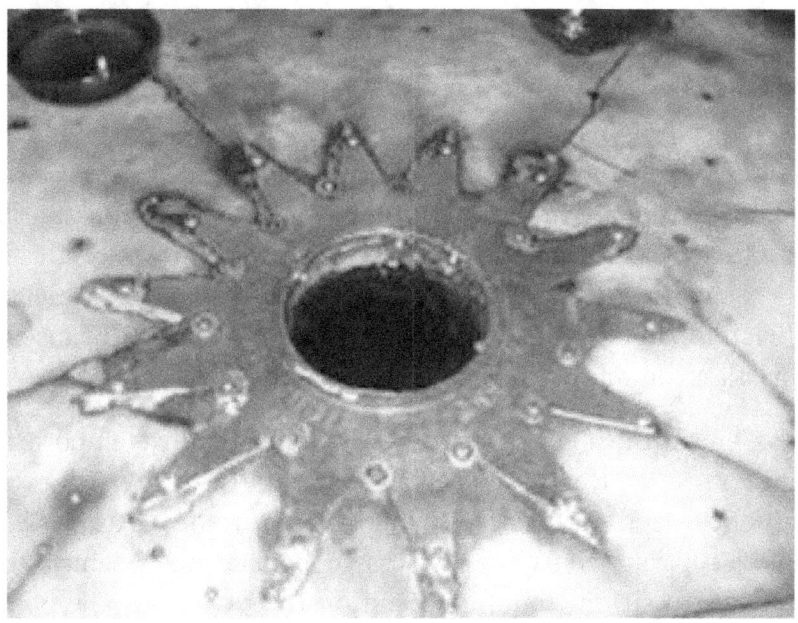

Kamil, the Arab Christian not yet 30 years old, is all enthusiasm for his job of enlightenment, fully motivated to convey his knowledge to us. Inside the cave he explains the 14-point silver star, the size of a basket ball, inlaid into the stone floor exactly where the birth took place. With a sense of awe, he conveys: "King David was born fourteen generations after Adam, and Jesus fourteen generations after David," implying that things like this cannot be made up by tricksters.

He further explains that as Christianity gained momentum in the first hundred years, converts flocked to the cave, establishing an unbroken verbal legacy regarding the birth place.

Kamil then adds – for good measure - that the Roman's did not like the riff raft coming to the cave and to dissuade the Christian pilgrims "Rome" installed a pagan alter inside. This too is documented within Roman journals, and hence Kamil assures us that the silver star marks the actual birth place

Roman suppression of Christian pilgrims ended when in the 300's the Roman Emperor Constantine embraced Christianity – after Arminia. Along with his devout mother, Constantine travelled to Palestine, visited the nativity cave, and built the world's earliest Christian church above the cave complex. This officially made Bethlehem a Christian destination and caused a Christian community to spring up around it.

Constantine's church becomes Greek Orthodox, temporarily squeezing the Roman Catholics out of the action. But the Catholics send Franciscan monks in with the Crusaders to build a separate church right next to Constantine's, which also manages to sit on top of one end of the cave. At some point, somehow, as usual, the Armenian Christians have a say in the matter and even they get a corner of the Greek church to call their own. This corner is, of course, also above the cave. The Catholics claim Jesus born on December 25th, the Orthodox January 6th and the Armenian's, again, January 25th, so together they have both the cave and the birth anniversaries covered.

Phew!

Bethlehem, today with a regional population of 200,000, is visible from Jerusalem. It stands a Christian city sandwiched between the Jewish and Moslem worlds.

But this tour of the birth place was not to be the telling experience of the afternoon. Instead the fate of a young Muslim boy took center stage.

Standing outside of the two churches, listening to Kamil describe a few last things – including his difficult life as a Palestinian Christian – a small, dark boy comes up a set of steps wanting to sell me a piece of gum. I wave him off and continue to focus on Kamil.

Suddenly the boy's father appears out of nowhere verbally attacking the son, finally kicking him in the knee and then running off. The child of six or seven collapses on the steps crying in agony. After a minute, while still howling in pain, he begins to work his way down the treacherous set of perhaps 40 stone stairs.

We move down the stairs as well, not to follow the boy, but to meet our driver who will fetch us below. On the street, Kamil explains that Muslims live a violent life, and that nothing in these West Bank towns curbs this as there is no controlling legal authority to cause order; it's a jungle existence.

Suddenly the father re-appears top of the steps and the boy claws himself up towards the father screaming in hatred, real defiance. The father comes down, threatens to kick the boy again but does not and the back and forth screaming continues.

My wife and daughters fear that another kick will send the boy down the stone stairs to his death, and a quiet appeal to Kamil is made about doing something. But he warns not to go near the situation, else it turns on us. *Kamil himself stands heartbroken, ashamed that this Bethlehem world - his world – operates with no civilized standards, and that this fact plays out in front of our eyes.*

Kamil: *Someday the Christians will all be gone.*

Apparently, after the six-day war in 1967, when Israel occupied the West Bank territory, Bethlehem – a West Bank town - was offered a special chance to join Israel. At the time Bethlehem - 80% Christian though Palestinian Arabs by race - turned down the offer. The Christian Palestinians in Bethlehem decided to maintain solidarity with their fellow Muslim cousins in other West Bank towns. Since then, Christian Palestinians fled due to continual chaos so that today Bethlehem is 80% Muslim and only 20% Christian… and sinking fast.

Fending for his Arab race, Kamil stresses that Arabs are good people; it is Islam that conditions their hate and violence.

Back in the van, Kamil opens up to us, points out a Christian school for girls explaining that woman mean nothing to Muslims and that Muslim children are taught nothing but garbage and hate.

Other than his parents, all of Kamil's extended family members have emigrated to places like Columbia. His sister in Florida is his great hope to get out.

Tel Aviv

Originally, I was on the fence about going to the "cement and steel" city of Tel Aviv, but Moti insisted.

Moti: *Only there can you understand the story of modern Israel.*

But first a stop at Moti's house. We meet his dog and eight cats, and his 20-year old son currently in the army. In Israel, one serves at 19 for two years prior to going to college. Moti's wife, who Moti adores, is out.

Moti: *These days not everyone serves. This is not good. When I served, I served the country. I don't want to serve slackers.*

Moti's son is smart and handsome, and he takes over as host showing us their small bomb shelter in the basement. After thirty minutes we climb back into Moti's Range Rover and head west to Tel Aviv.

Tel Aviv, a sky rise city today, did not exist one hundred years ago. Back then one found only sand dunes there. I doubt any city of this magnitude has a similar situation of no deep historical legacy whatsoever.

In contrast, just a few miles south, Jaffa rests, an ancient port city from Canaanite times. The Jaffa Gate in old Jerusalem once opened to a road that led to Jaffa on the Mediterranean coast. This biblical road became highway 1 today.

Moti's plan makes Jaffa the first stop, then the flea market, then the National Museum.

Jaffa

From what I can tell, every era of mankind touched Jaffa, from the Canaanites to the Egyptians to the Romans to Napoleon. When Napoleon attacked Egypt – for no good reason actually – he marched north and took Jaffa as well, 4,000 surrendered. When asked what to do with 4,000, the young, 28-year old general ordered them shot.

Today old Jaffa and new Tel Aviv meet, and in this no man's land one finds a large, permanent flea market that extends for many streets. We arrive at noon on a Friday in late December, sunny and 65 Degrees, as all of Tel Aviv trudges through the bazar shops. Remember the Jewish day of worship is Saturday, so the Israelis weekend spans Friday and Saturday, back to work on Sunday.

Moti: *For lunch I will take you to my favorite place. Do you like pieta bread?*

Somewhere in the heart of the bazaar a crowd lines up three deep against a long street-side serving display filled with goodies, to order these cooked pieta sandwiches, and we finally get ours: "salty cheese and hard boiled eggs, heated up". Somehow I am not surprised that this is Moti's favorite place.

A block further down I notice a bar with tables on the street with room for the five of us so I grab the spot as Moti goes in for beers,

Moti: *They won't serve us. We didn't buy our food from them. They are Arabs.*

Quickly eating our pieta concoctions, we soon find another bar, this one packed outside, so we go in for beers at the bar.

The National Museum

Moti: *Now you will learn. We go to the National Museum.*

In 1900 there was no Tel Aviv, just sand dunes left by years of Mediterranean storms. The creation of Tel Aviv, and the State of Israel are coupled together, and both of these amazing achievements are concisely presented at the National Museum in the center of Tel Aviv.

The museum lives in one of the original houses built at the city's founding.

Moti: *Buy your tickets and first see the short film in English. I will be out front at 2:30.*

Here is what I learned:

Way back in the late 1800's *Theodor Herzel* from Germany postulated the concept of a Jewish State in a book called **Altneuland** (old new land). Rather than Jews living as minorities in other countries they would come together and prosper as one concentrated entity, just like other nation states, a self-evident idea called "Zionism" never suggested before.

The last Jewish state fell to the Romans 2,000 years back, so the Herzel idea caught the fancy of many. In 1909 a group of sixty families living in Jaffa amongst Arab and Turkish majorities decided to try it. They bought empty land a few miles north on the beach, and laid out a plan for a city with wide roads, in the modern European style, and by lot, each family was assigned a building parcel.

And they built their little town, calling it *Tel Aviv*. Tel, in Hebrew, meaning *a man made hill built on ancient ground*, and Aviv meaning *spring* – i.e. antiquity rejuvenated. Then as Europe heated up after World War I, Jews by the thousands started moving to this unique city of Jews.

Recall from the timeline presented a few pages back, that until World War I, the Ottomans - who controlled Palestine for 500 years - were tolerant of Muslims, Jews and Christians. The same proved true after World Was I when Britain governed the area. So in its own right, in the first half of the 1900's, the Palestine area held attraction for Jews.

Many came from communist Russia with some embracing socialism, the idea behind the first Kibbutz's. These Eastern European participants introduced more radical aspirations. Many of today's Hasidic people are of Eastern European stock.

Conversely, from the get go, Tel Aviv, founded during the Kibbutz era, represented a more secular, western European mentality. In the late 1930's Tel Aviv reached 100,000 souls; today the number stands at half a million.

David Ben-Gurion

Then came the holocaust and World War II, and by 1947 worldwide support for a Jewish nation state grew in response. A United Nation's resolution carved out land for this to happen triggering Arab indignation. But the project went forward.

In 1948, under the leadership of *David Ben-Gurion* - the Israelis George Washington - the independence trigger was pulled, the declaration signed in the very house now hosting the museum. Arab armies from many countries attacked that very day.

Though I have read the detail, I have no idea how the Israelis' pulled this off.

Hardened survivors from the holocaust, they only had the 1946 to 1948 period to prepare for the coming Arab onslaught, raising money from America and elsewhere, grabbing huge stores of left over armaments from the war, and organizing a citizen army - of just 35,000 - into a command structure, one capable of going on the offensive against Arab troops once trained under the British.

This achievement of preparedness, and the crushing victory by numerous Israelis commanders over their adversaries is why David Ben-Gurion is certainly the modern day Washington.

Woman from a kibbutz train for war.

Going Home

We are at the end of the day, and the trip, and I tell Moti that I want to return to the Wailing Wall to witness the action during the Shabbat.

The Shabbat – literally meaning "ceasing" – begins Friday at dusk, lasting until dusk on Saturday. The practice comes from the biblical law to cease work at dusk on the sixth day and rest on the seventh. If one is Shabbat observant, at dusk one refrains from activities like driving, making phone calls and using things requiring electricity. One's food is prepared in advance.

Moti: *We will have to hurry. I cannot drive in the old city during Shabbat.*

I say that he can just drop us off at the Jaffa gate and we can walk in.

Moti: *No, I will drive you close and wait outside the Dung gate and drive you back to the hotel.*

I realize that this being the end of our time together that Moti wants to finish things properly so I agree. We are in a traffic jam approaching Jerusalem and this makes things tight for the ambitious plan. Moti asks another driver to roll down his window.

Moti: *When is Shabbat?*

The driver says: 4:10. Moti hates the answer and looks at me:

Moti: *4:10, that can't be. Look at the sun, there's too much light left.*

He inches up to another driver and gets the same answer. Still not buying it he calls somebody who confirms 4:10.

Moti: *We will make it.*

And we did. The tank driver whisked us through the old city streets without hitting one pedestrian and dropped us in front of the metal detectors leading to the Wailing Wall complex.

Moti: *I'll be outside the gate.*

There are two metal detectors, and two lines of one hundred persons each waiting to get in, one line for men the other for women. The lines move quickly.

As I get close I notice that Hasidics are coming down a flight of stairs right before the detectors, cutting the line. Then more Hasidics, whole families cutting the line. Other than myself, the line is all Jews as far as I can tell, all the men wearing orthodox black hats or yarmulkes.

I am amazed that no one says anything about this level of rudeness. Finally I experience the paradox regular Jews live with: they can't stand the Hasidics, but they enable them every step of the way.

Oh well. I don't live here.

Inside, down at the Wailing Wall, it is 40 people deep, the men dressed in black, the woman showing Israelis blue. Quite a scene!

We Americans lean on the ramp walls watching the people flock to the demarcation areas but we don't go further.

Finally, back at the King David Hotel, after a warm goodbye with Moti, I ponder: What would have happened if not for him?

Inside the hotel we sit for the Shabbat dinner the King David kitchen prepared earlier that day, then to bed, up at 4:00 AM to catch the 7:30 AM British Air flight out of *Ben Gurion Airport.*

Shalom!

www.ingramcontent.com/pod-product-compliance
Lightning Source LLC
Chambersburg PA
CBHW071223070526
44584CB00019B/3129